THE BEAUTY
OF
CURVED SPACE

STEPHEN LINSTEADT

GLASS LYRE PRESS

Copyright © 2015 Stephen Linsteadt
Paperback ISBN: 978-1-941783-14-6

All rights reserved: except for the purpose of quoting brief passages for review, no part of this book may be reproduced or transmitted in any form or by any means, electronic or mechanical, including photocopying, recording, or by any information storage and retrieval system, without permission in writing from the publisher.

Cover art ("Unknown Woman 1979") and interior illustrations by Stephen Linsteadt
Design & layout: Steven Asmussen
Copyediting: Linda E. Kim
Author Photo: Maria Elena Boekemeyer

Glass Lyre Press, LLC
P.O. Box 2693
Glenview, IL 60026

www.GlassLyrePress.com

Contents

Both Sides of Beauty	7
Feminine Environment	8
Raised by a Woman in Disguise	9
Barcelona	10
An Unecessary Detour	12
Together on Opposite Sides of the Bed	13
Drifting on Paint	14
While You Sleep	16
Paying the Price for Joy	17
I See Things	18
Finding My Way on a Flat Canvas	20
I Made Love to Your Voice	21
Taking Mojave with Me	22
Painting Between Shores	25
Chocolates	28
Voices in the Studio	31
Bouquet	34
Don't Get Caught Laughing	36
The Line Whisperer	37
Painting on Drums	38
Shaman on a Trip	39
The Habit of Contrast	41
Between Dreams	42
Before the Magic Mirror	43
Painting with Turpentine and a Rag	45
Crown of Honeycomb	48
Signs Left by Calvino	50
The Arousal of Venus and Jupiter	51
Who	52
Satisfaction	54
The Impertinence of Jupiter	55
A Woman Who Loved Me	56

Participation Mystique	57
Untraceable	58
On Pont D'Avignon	59
Canal du Midi	61
Autumn Composition	63
Saint-Rémy de Provence	64
Songs	66
Slipping on Wet Paint	67
Unicorn in the Mirror	68
Self Portrait	69
Mirrors	70
The Next Moment	72
The Secret Language of Irises	74
Going Through Tubes of Paint	75
A Strange Precession	77
Hope Between Chaos	78
Acknowledgments	81
About the Author	83

Both Sides of Beauty

You ask me to help you
unfasten your favorite necklace
and then return it to your special box.

I hold the mirror.

You put on my shirt unbuttoned to expose
the bitter sweet scent of virginity
drawing me close to your warmth.

You hold my arm

then ask if you are my soul desire
or do I long for the Giver of the jewels:
my Things and apparent free will.

Reconciled by the sixth sense
and the play of subtle glances
I follow you to the rose-covered trellis
lay next to you
on a flower-strewn bed.

You press my cheek against your breast
where I lay and wait for the cunning huntress
to turn me inwards upon myself.

Feminine Environment

The soul of the feminine
my constant companion:

the goddess that inspires creativity,

the one who is numinous by her virtue
and sweet scent,

The Unknown Woman who walks beside me
in my dreams along a river bank and leaves me
mystified and alone when I awake.

She is my teacher, smiling at me
through my wife's eyes; the natural woman
searching for an understanding partner.

But the one I worry about the most
is Spider Woman, coming to say,
Hey you, human beings, out of the pool.
Look what you have done to the water.

Raised by a Woman in Disguise

I am the illicit son
of Mars and the Vestal Virgin

I am the illicit son
whose twin was set adrift to Nod

I am the illicit son
swallowed by darkness at the end of each day

I am the illicit son
the predator who seduced the unsuspecting red

I am the illicit son
who rarely howls

I am the illicit son
exhausting its prey in unrelenting confusion

I am the illicit son
the false prophet on the open steppes

I am the illicit son
mated for life to the moon

Barcelona

I

We made it to the last reading
of the Festival de Poesía in time to hear
a poet hiding behind the mask of human personality.
He read in Catalan so I could be wrong about the mask,
but girls like girls, like girls like a horse—
those things that escape notice,
like fuck rhythm, red crack bottom nipples,
red harlequin saxophone in the key of E
and *otra cosas.*

II

There is a mammoth behind you
in case you hadn't noticed.
I can see its tusks curling up
from your head.
That would explain my headache.
That, and Chantal's stars on my tongue.

A young girl draws attention to herself
in a white communion dress. The rest of us
are sunbathing in the park or strolling
with leashed dogs no larger than pigeons.
The smell of jasmine, spring sun,
the *Arc de Triomf* in the distance—
a monument to the end of decadence.

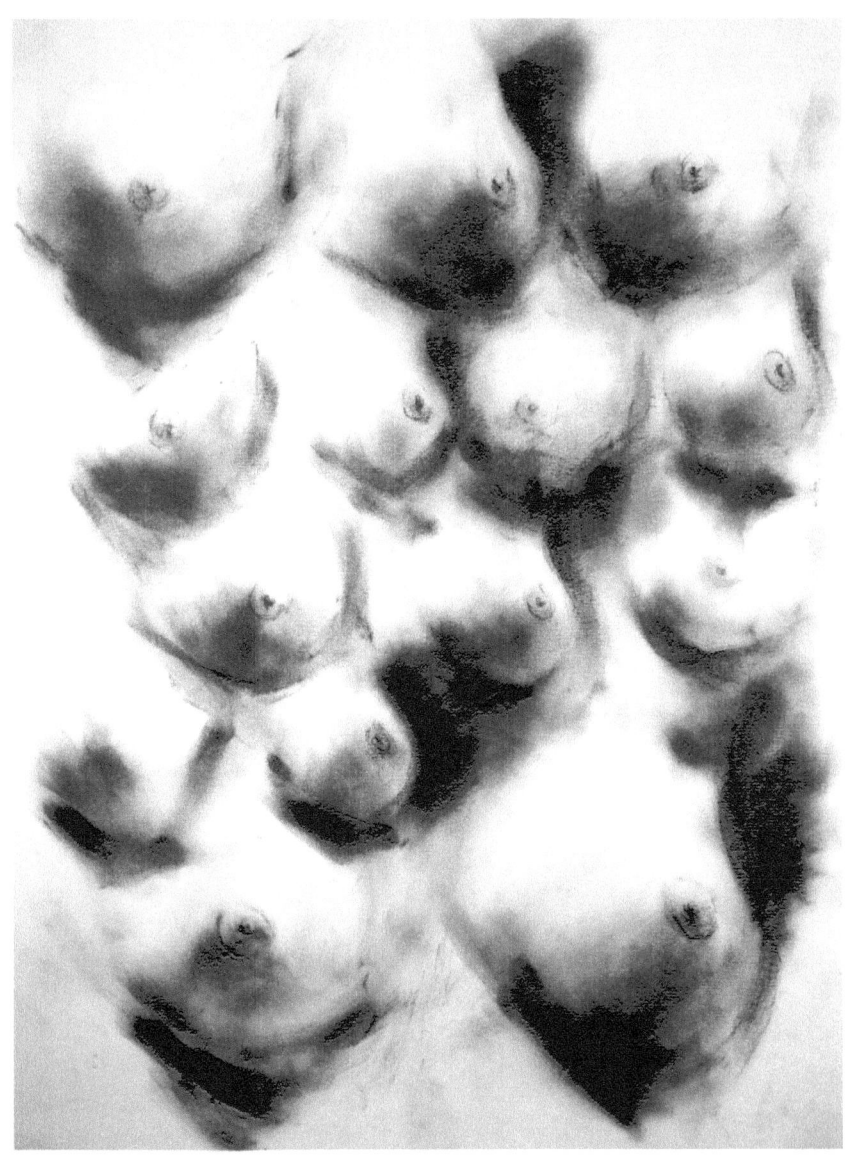

AN UNECESSARY DETOUR

Her breasts float to the surface.
I mistake their resurrection for an invitation
but they were only curious.

She stands dripping water as she steps
over me and out of the tub.

I'm left with bubbles that multiply into walls
of little breasts hiding a secret labyrinth
whose walls are dank and envious.

I leave the bathroom to find the sheets
pulled back from the bed.

Reclining against the pillows
her undressed body still moist
smells of Ylang Ylang.

Together on Opposite Sides of the Bed

The air conditioner kicks in
blankets stiffen
the sheets half dreaming

I want to make love to her
she is sound asleep

We have become parallel
bodies infinitely meeting
forever explaining each other

The incredible feeling of being
yourself all the way
through the foam of shared toothpaste

Drifting on Paint

The existentialism of shadows their paradox
like painting icebergs, the parts we don't see.

Waiting for shadows to step aside.

I hate it when mice show up in my dreams and cockroaches
take turns laughing, like everyone gets the joke but me.

I paint what I feel so I can struggle
with an audience, but they're too busy rehearsing their lines
as if everyone else is the more exciting person.†

My soul is busy transferring material of the outside world
into the interior—

I can't tell if I'm in the interior
floating on the essence of my life's experiences
or drifting on what's left over.

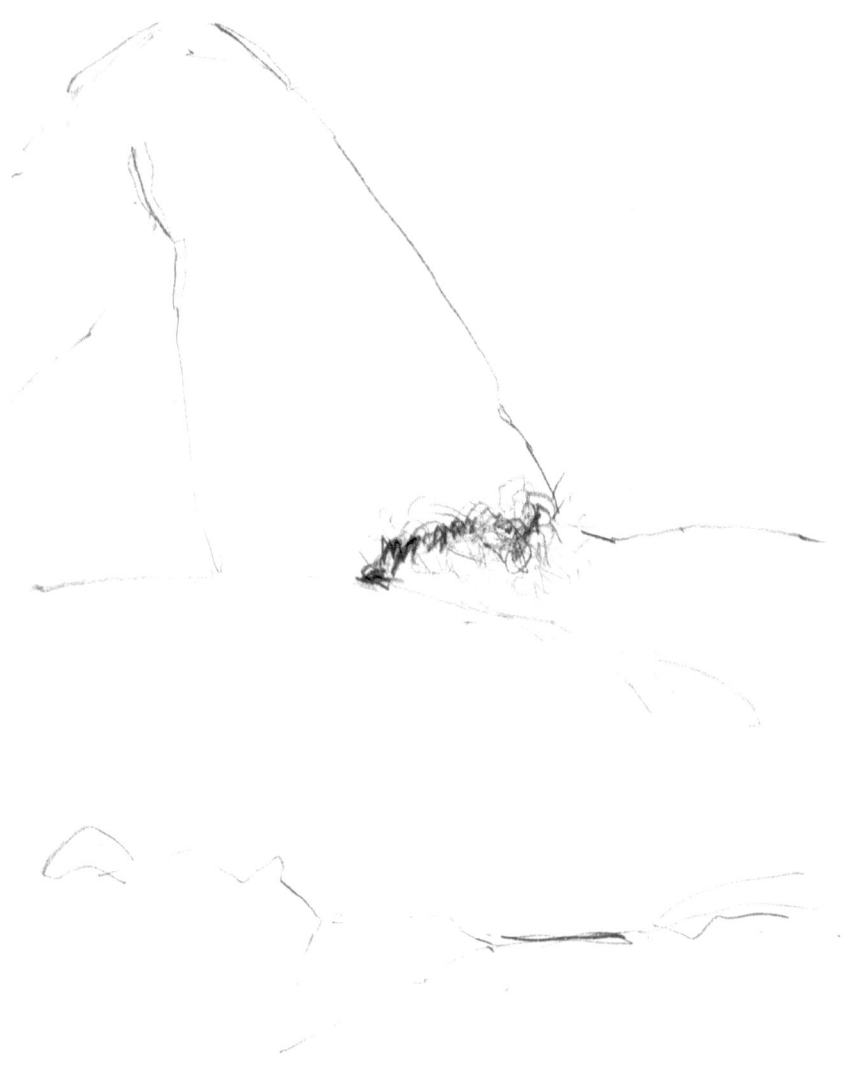

While You Sleep

I caress the round fragrant ridges
over your long back.

My hand travels many moles; a long and pleasant journey,
a safari of untamed expectations.

My fingertips find the base of twin dunes—
my heart races at the edge.

You roll over, eyes open—
my delirium nestles in your long curls
and though your face remains in shadow
your voice soothes my trembling
the way a rose captures the nightingale.

I am seized by an unfamiliar memory—
imprisoned by a singular heartbeat,
one infinite beat, an eternal pause opening to a field
where Rumi and Hafiz play soccer and laugh at my confusion.

The rose laughs.
The nightingale laughs.
The unknown face laughs.

You laugh as I catch my breath—
then smile.

† Interviews with Francis Bacon, by David Sylvester (Thames & Hudson 1987)

Paying the Price for Joy

Somersaults off the end of a swing
when joy was dangerous and bones were hard

before consciousness turned non-local
and falling off my bike was synchronistic.

In the hospital
characters in my dreams were animated by me alone.

My awake Self creates the illusion I am the victim
not the creator. The connecting thread, that Eros,

the goddess that plunges deep into shadows
where mermaids fathom the depth of a fleshy heart

and atoms are condensations of thought.
Even then, Isis would have to return the missing phallus,

the one flies dine on in the Egyptian sand.

In the shade of the erect
one could raise a white flag

to stand as a beacon of valor and hope.

When I came to, it was my mother's face I saw first,
not my father's

who reminded me later that men don't cry.

I See Things

no one else sees—
the schools no longer there;
the record store; the faces at the baseball field;
the girl with honey hair sitting on the old tin-can
   (the name we gave the short yellow school bus).

I hear voices no one else hears; friends
lost to leukemia and car accidents; those
appearing on a growing list at every reunion.

The houses have all vanished
but I still see them across the desert floor
like the elusive water shimmering
on burning asphalt.

My past is a ghost town,
a horizon into infinity,
an archaeological treasure beneath Wal-Mart and Costco.

I'm just driving through on my way to the future.

The mountains stay—they can see things
no one else sees.

Finding My Way on a Flat Canvas
after Robert Henri

I know when I'm lost
I scratch myself with the arrow of Eros
distilling the poison into singleness

The Hindoo state of abandoning the material
leaving an outline which may be deciphered
Traces of states more graceful flame up

My every thought registers envy with each brush stroke

Brushstrokes speak boldly or meagerly
Sometimes selfish sometimes generous

Lines carry messages magnifying all my uncertainties
Marks appear to stand stiff until movement passes through them
tracing the outlines of my fears

In my dreams I turn the canvas over
trace the residue a mirror image
an anti-self below the surface
as if repetition will matter

but the hounds have lost the scent
and my brushes have grown blurry

I Made Love to Your Voice

this morning
as you read aloud
Neruda and Petit.

I wanted to kiss your poetry,
hold hands with your hair.

That was enough
for a lifetime.

Taking Mojave with Me

Their souls imprisoned behind bark
for seven hundred years,
a redwood forest casts shadows indifferent
to my last enemy
and the thousand ills of fate.

Mendocino coast, the last splash
of Lemurian lush.

I know her ferns and foliage
from Mojave fossils
and bleached bones stacked
like driftwood
on dry crustaceous shores.

Living in the desert
is bad feng shui.

But it is home to my memories,
the ones that never bloom
no matter how much rain pours on badlands.

I listen stubbornly for extinct whispers at dusk
when my subconscious scampers on the surface.

Tumbleweed like trees don't care
about my journey to enlightenment.

So I ride dinosaurs with wings and ask sea urchins
for permission to move to the ocean
where I can swim in my future and hope
shadows and the waves of fate
can't find me.

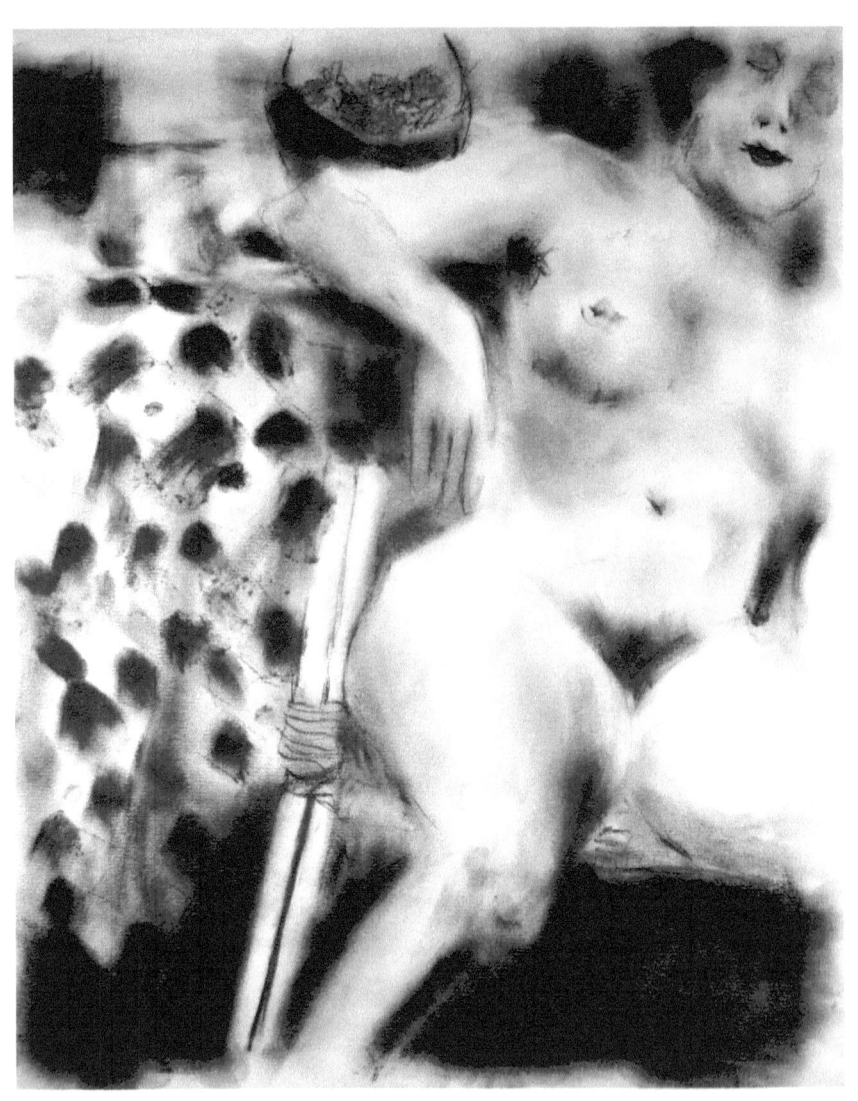

Painting Between Shores

The end of my brush traces old scars
below the edges of bones

(Oh I want to see them:
7 stitches in the forehead for calling me a girl.
You ran when I picked up a rock then turned around in time to catch it in the skull.
I bruised my brain once when I rode into a truck.)

Half in, half out
       these scars breathe a confession

when I stand in a certain light

sifting through erasures
to find my exiled slave.

(Like the blood my neighbor's wife wiped away
after she sat on my lap at a dinner party

       wanting to catch her husband's attention.)

Now I make the canvas bleed—

the swamp cooler runs out of water again and I'm down to my shorts.

Fluorescent tubes spoil the backlighting.

Sand pounds on the door.

At my feet a turpentine soaked rag,
a sail,
a loadstone,
the only way back to the surface.

I almost forgot her nakedness
transposed to the canvas—

her breasts hoping for re-election
wave to the crowd.

but the model, unaware,
dresses then leaves.

Chocolates

Some grump once said,
Life is like a box of chocolates.

I think he meant some relationships
are palatable, adorable, even luscious
while others horrid, gooey or artificial.

That never stopped me
from eating whole boxes
in one sitting, making me
a connoisseur of sorts.

I now know all about childhood gummy bears
and adolescent licorice and their premature
bursts of ingratitude—fruit-filled juiciness
teasing and stingy.

I used to enjoy inner moistness wrapped
in thin layers of innocent kisses—
clarified and resuscitated, but later discovered
they were emulsified and tart, yet
inconsistently caramel.

Cocoa and coconut looked good
but they were nuts all the way down.

I got sick once on pomegranate suitcases
stuffed with borderline psychosis.

Worst of all were pregnant pralines
delivering lies in divorce court
along with insulin resistant alimony payments
wrapped in salt water taffy.

A new assortment arrived from Chile—
white chocolate with swirls
that made my almonds cluster
and melted slowly in my mouth—
pure cane sugar, an aphrodisiac
like electric shock treatment.
It caused my past to roll onto the floor
but I left the mess intoxicated.

Eventually, I learned to check ingredients
ahead of time for allergic reactions.

I want you to taste the enclosed.
They're hand-made, top-shelf,
for the most discerning.

I thought of you immediately.
After all, you're a professional
and will appreciate dark
Jasmine Tea Truffles
I'm sure.

They taste like our relationship—
a little bitter
to keep you from drowning
in sweet.

Voices in the Studio

She stood behind me while I painted,
then commented on my work
sending me out of my body.

*Good god, do you know what it's like
to have voices suddenly talking behind your head?*

Welcome to my world, she says.

Brown paint oozes like a herd of antelope
churning the landscape.

Skeleton Woman drinks cupfuls of green tears
as an unearthly chant rises from the surface...

*We don't have a word for 'tin'
that's why we call him the Zinc Man.*

I thought you left, I say. *Really,
I need to concentrate.*

But I'm bored as an oyster.

My Palette falls in the painting
like the salt mill that grinds in the ocean.

He never hides things for his convenience
or to be a delicatessen. He changed
the curse of my life.

I turn to beg for silence
but I find myself alone.

I let the voices percolate from the canvas
and echo through the studio.

Bouquet

The hairs on her neck
sweet and softly delicate
in silence beg for a kiss.

I laugh and insist she will notice.

Believing permission is not required
they tell me to wait until she looks away.

I ponder the invitation
and kiss her on the mouth
thinking it is the better prize.

Her lips admonish me to ask her eyes—
next time,
who are flattered, then explain:
the one you seek dwells behind
in shadows between a land forgotten
where you may not follow
(in your present form)
as long as you insist on kissing little hairs
and stealing parted lips.

Forehead to forehead
I glimpse the light of her
in a closet where expectant
memories hang.

I've come courting with a
bouquet of amnesia
that leaves me staring
at my reflection,
unsure—
*am I pursuing or
am I pursued?*

Don't Get Caught Laughing

I was five when the swing set tipped over
from too much laughter.

I was stoic after that
afraid optimism was charged with static.

Like a mockingbird I go through the motions.

Flying beyond myself attracts swing sets.

My heart dares me to let go, to do somersaults
into the smile of uncertainty.

My mind is afraid I'll break my neck
but I'm dying anyway.

The Line Whisperer

Lines aren't just architectural
without variation in thickness. Lines have a life,
a beginning and an end. They have joys and sorrows
in between. Like the line that contours a woman's hip,
it tells us it is hip by its proportion and context.

The line speaks through its undulations of her many lovers,
her aspirations, disappointments, and regrets.

The painter's lines are the syllables in the poet's verse, the adjectives
of feeling, the heroes and the villains.

The line-whisperer knows better
the story told in marks and scratches.

Painting on Drums

Each new song is the sound of paint
between the ridges,

tangled in uncensored ways
through my personality.

I hear coyotes like babies
behind the yurt, in their howls.

Sixteen Pueblo medicine men died in 1998—
they were no longer needed.

The cop's wife told me she found
his stash of satin underwear for my first wife.

Like the executioner,
I try to amputate my hand from the brush.

But it's too late, I've already dragged
too many bones into the canvas.

Shaman on a Trip

Light didn't bend
until Einstein said it must
and we invented equations to agree.

Light travelled without restriction
until we clocked it.

She dreamt about eagles
and eagles circled above her car
when she left for the airport.

She looked forward to sleeping
on the plane.

A voice announced her name over the loudspeaker—

she had been upgraded to first class.

The Cosmos continues to expand
as long as the Hubble telescope peers into space.

The Habit of Contrast

His freshly painted ballerina poses in red
between ocher walls and mirrors
ornate in crimsons and blues.

In the maze of infinite reflections
each iteration dispenses other dancers
in receding halls—frozen memories
whose circumstances crystallize, if only
in her mind.

A distant recollection wants to know
who told the model
she was loved and the world was good,
why she keeps the difficult story alive
inside her head.

The model squints through smoke of hash
while the dancer laughs:
we're only brushstrokes of color
lulled to sleep by the contrast,
left deaf to the secret symphony
calling us to dance.

Between Dreams

I am not a woman, not a man

I slip through the juices like a surging wave
like a dolphin surfing on the foam of laughter

I am the sigh of a dream
longing to be remembered

Before the Magic Mirror

The mirror of my mind
refuses to show my true reflection—
it shimmers only glimpses of epitaphs
and ghostly proclamations—
self imposed dogmas
fashioned out of shaving cream.

This dull inner vision
tricks me to believe
I am something else
entirely—a reflection distorted
by the varnish of
pomegranate juice
promised seeds of pleasure
and their bitter pulpy flesh.

I never consider wiping the mirror
so I go on slicing my face to pieces—
too vain to grow a beard.

Painting with Turpentine and a Rag

That first brush stroke on a blank canvas,
that great hesitation, where reason is abandoned
long enough to allow reflexes to have their way
and the brush to choose its own palette.

The fear lies in subsequent interpretations,
the lingering sense of judgment.

Brush strokes are vulnerable when left alone.

The temptation is to mould drops and splashes
into houses or trees, something conforming,
recognizable by an imaginary audience.

The art critics will want to write an article
causing me to regret I didn't think of sheep
in tanks of formaldehyde
or giant purple poodles.

So I scrape out the childish scene of trees
with turpentine and a rag
and start over.

The blank canvas stretched over my ego
is stained by all my false starts.
It sits like a neon sign for the world to know
I was born without an original thought.

When I close my eyes and paint in the dark
the canvas fills with possibilities.

Brush strokes sing in fluid vermilion and crimson,
the stops and starts.

The delicate strokes and the heavy ones
keep time to the harmony of that moment,

and only that moment.

An unearthly chant rises from the surface
like jewels from a flood, receding imperceptively,
remaining only in my mind.

Another blank canvas is waiting.

Crown of Honeycomb

She waits and watches
as I busy about
collecting experiences from matter;
lifetimes of learning to extract the essence
from the moment.

She waits for my sorrows
to distil into nectar
and ferment the mead of honeymoon.

She waits for the scent of her substance
to transform my yearning
into a winged being of fire.

She wears a crown of honeycomb
and waits.

SIGNS LEFT BY CALVINO
after Italo Calvino

The erasure of my mark
is not the same as the negation of self.
It means I am free to have an opinion.

It also allows others to have an opinion
so I scatter false marks on the canvas
as decoys.

A line has a beginning and an end—

there is always a variation of thickness in between,
the way joy and sorrow add dimension to fate.

Lines tend to superimpose one upon the other
as everyone invariably leaves their mark
in a general thinness to each other.

Lines bend through the curvature of space
especially in the voids.

Lines tend to have an outside and an inside
       a conscious aspect
       and an unconscious one.

The expectation of new lines
the addiction.

† Cosmicomics, "A Sign in Space"

The Arousal of Venus and Jupiter

Venus and Jupiter vie for your approval
beneath the crescent smile encouraging
soft lips across velvet saucers.

Rapturous suckles mix with warm scented mosses—
rhythmic pulses invites a heat scented frenzy of sweat
accompanied by a chorus sizzling on hot sand.

The throbbing in your neck proclaims a warm desire—
kindles to flame as two hearts devour one another and vanish
on a warm summer breeze
to etch an eternity into a single moment.

Who

is waiting
to know me
(I barely know myself)

who
told the wolf
to become dog
that humans needed a friend
someone to teach and guide them
knowing they are mostly unteachable
and unguidable

but who
already knew this
and did so anyway

who
is kidding who

Satisfaction

Light shimmers as it cascades across linen
revealing refulgence of glowing skin
through an open blouse. Buttons, like beacons, dance
against their moors the way a morning breeze welcomes
soft air through its folds.

Occupied with reminiscence, she stands,
not noticing a pensive gaze.

Perhaps the Tylenol bottle and paper coffee cup
reflect the night she spent and now regrets.

Why won't you at least look at me?

Something I said or left unsatisfied?

The first rays of morning sun glare and I wish
she were a waterfall of light and every cell a twinkle
falling into endless satisfaction.

The Impertinence of Jupiter

The Moon didn't mind so much
when Pisces entangled her fullness
in a reflection of a brighter source
but still, in her own right
she was the mistress
in which the Sun
could have a private conversation.

What really got her
was the impertinence of Jupiter
who naturally barged in
that bastard
that arrogant spot light.

So she waxed on for a few more days
then left altogether
with the tides.

We haven't seen her
for a couple weeks.

A Woman Who Loved Me

All the vanilla ice cream I could eat
while you read the editorial pages,
Ehrlichman and Nixon—
hours of senate hearings on the zenith.

I waited by stacked cases of empty Dr Pepper bottles
for warm fresh biscuits, wiping steam
off the back kitchen window
until I could see your face—
a smiling reflection.

Participation Mystique

I started out wanting to paint Truth,
plainly, without prejudice.

But like Holbein, we don't want to see
what lies behind the jewel laden mosaic.

Gray Antelope commanded a cripple
to pick up corn scattered on the floor and
to bring it to him without crutches—and he did.

The clothespin goddess
with the four phases of the moon chanted
while Hanne played her crystal bowls.

Lizards with missing tails
crowd me in the studio. Truth
poses in the dark, dressing, then leaving,
before I can turn the lights back on.

Untraceable

Eager to transcend into untraceable consciousness
she hears the thought *I am nothing*
penetrate the emptiness
shattering her untraceableness to pieces
and suddenly
her image is again before the mirror
and another day lies before her
with all its possibilities and remembrances
the thing she tries to forget

It's that thing
the irritation of purpose and meaning
as if asked to do something
then forgot to remember
when forgetting is the oblivion
the paradox of actionless action
the annoyance of doing nothing
trying hard to be famously infamous
pretending not to notice
when expectations disappoint
and she's back to the unbearable fullness
of feeling empty

On Pont d'Avignon

you regret your past and find comfort
in a rose petal you find
on the steps to Bénézet's Bridge.

You have crossed many bridges
with your red umbrella,

this one impassable,
       three quarters destroyed by the King
          in the siege of twelve-twenty-six.

The villagers built a new bridge above the old, the way
you build new dreams
from the mortar of your past.

You laugh and point to a man
wearing a hat of flowers.

The Alterarosa in the Palais des Papes;
your linen dress unable to conceal
you against the background sun.

We argue about the color of Audacieuse 21.

I repeated what you said
only with more words.

I try to remember the Gnostic rose.

The invaders were already inside the walls
when the ramparts crumbled in loyalty to the exiled.

The cooing of pigeons standing on the altar
echo with gold coins strewn
by guilt across the chapel floor;
        a tithing for a palace.

Why do you have tears in your eyes,
you were over it a minute ago?

CANAL DU MIDI

The hoopoe chimes
in the midday sun silencing
church bells nearby.

A nightingale echoes the song
that reverberates like smoke signals
across hilltops.

A cloud suspended between
the walls of a stained glass birdcage
has lost its voice.

It sings a silent song
about fire in the forest
sparked with flint of reason.

The Canal du Midi promises
golden bells sunk beneath its surface—
when I finally learn to listen.

Autumn Composition

lightning cracks through rain
but you stay in the pool
the smell
oh the smell
you say
and sink beneath the steam

bursts of yellow cottonwood leaves
set free over sulfur pools
before a storm front timpani

your smile floats to the surface
enchanted by the orchestra
a concerto for two

SAINT-RÉMY DE PROVENCE

A whale of rock jumps out of the land
and freezes above the earth;
the backdrop to "Starry Night"
painted close to where green bathed
the artist's vision in a yellow
        tainted room.

The scent of Languedoc
still warm about your neck.

Thunder uncoils over the night.

Rain on my umbrella
drops of deep mystery. Madness in May
only warm iris blossoms understand.

Their light whispers
and won't hold still.

You can't complain I'm singing
        this is an asylum.

And where are the human beings
who once lived in the olive groves?

We were compelled to keep our distance
        from the chapel.

Pigeons cooed then waited
for the echo to reverberate
off its stained glass walls.

Songs

The creek that carves through the roots of the oak
sings its song in staccato to the birds,
their mating squawks, and the pitch of insects—
a symphony to my ears, unexpected,
as if I arrived late to the music hall.

Do birds, dragonflies, and croaking frogs
also hear their song or are human beings
unique in their awareness?

When I am preoccupied does the song still play?
Do other forests, unheard by human ears, sing as beautifully?

And if I pray for silence
from the deaf and mute of my everydayness
will I hear the song from the balcony of the stars?
Is that the reason for their smile or is their twinkle
the reflection off their opera glass?

Perhaps they have not gathered to watch
my life as I suppose. Perhaps I am only a stagehand
taking bows before a show more grand.

Slipping on Wet Paint

Existentialists make better painters

Wet paint oozes between their psychology

Why Turner never grasped his own atmosphere
and Rothko abandoned himself in one way
fields of colour

Perhaps they had a secret behind their painting
a cigarette before they started
a glass of wine
a monk on a CD

I only have sandstorms outside
and the hours I sit and look at empty canvases

Wrestling for meaning a match Warhol forfeited
one Duchamp mocked with androgyny

Admittedly Van Gogh never captured light
moving through cypress

But I can always count on the wind to blow

Unicorn in the Mirror

I have often tried to capture
the invisible Unicorn,
hoping to lure it with pomegranates
into my mind's fenced-in pen.

I once dreamt I saw a glimpse of white mane
in the reflection of a mirror held by a virgin,
one whose purity of heart had risen
above false promises.

Oh, how I long for that mirror
and the image of the Unknown Woman
upon its still, calm pool.

Self Portrait

I pretend to know who I am
but the accidents in paint
have their own proposals
forcing me to adopt a new context.

I paint until I can no longer find myself—
consciousness parades in pigment
like ticker tape through Dante's dark wood.

Each brushstroke a different fragment—
a nuance of emotions repressed.

Each line a new revelation,
a mystic curve or splash—
continually renewing myself
at the end of the brush.

I tend to hide behind the canvas
putting myself back together without the lies.

The more I paint the less I know.

Mirrors

We smile and bow before the mirror
Illuminating our costume,
Blocking from our view
The hands of the Puppeteer,
Whose animating strings dance
Our existence into being

While we lament the apparent
Entanglement of our dreadful roles,
The martyr, the villain—
The characters we play—
The mirror giggles
Knowing from its "unprovable
Innermost depths"* it is ultra thin
As an infinitesimal illusion
And if we would only adjust our
Depth of vision, we would realize
The Puppeteer is a Mannequin,
Without script, led only
By our applause

* Rilke – notebook entry, early November 1910

The Next Moment

Oh the euphoria
when the first drop of you courses
through my blood
and the complexities of life vanish
and I am bodiless and weightless
without past or future
inebriated beyond recognition
beyond existence
beyond rapture
beyond the thought:
    this won't last.

The Secret Language of Irises

Along the canal built to connect
the ocean with the sea, I found a path
unknown where human voices muffle in the hulls.

My heart filled with the song of nightingale
in the plane trees on the river's edge, the cooing of
two black swans, and the waving of water flags
along the shore.

I paused to watch swans exchange subtle glances.

A dragonfly appeared to my relaxing eyes—her iridescent
wings of Iridos recorded my dreams and delivered them
as rainbows to tiny spirits on the other side.

My wishes burst into yellow blossoms in the silent
language of Irises.

The wings of dragonfly matched the spectral
circles of my eyes—a constant reminder
that what I think reflects on the water's surface.

I surrendered to the rhythm of the spirals
and followed the river beyond ocean and sea
and drank deeply.

Going Through Tubes of Paint

When I was young and had surplus energy
I painted women voluptuous with smiles wanting
like de Kooning's women
spread across the canvas dripping.

When relationships failed
I painted women fractured
disassembled like Larry Rivers'
Parts of the Face.

When I felt my isolation too large
I painted Bacon's figures wrestling,
a stage where spotlights cast doubt on the effort.

Palace interiors later dripped from my brush
their grand halls dimly lit by all knowing chandeliers
in the empty rooms of my mind where the future rehearsed
and the past took bows.

Palaces became cathedrals to mock my altar
where choirboys sang lullabies out of tune
but the women always returned
lines and scrawls had memorized their form.

Through the layers of pigment alembics became breasts
landscapes: hips and curves rounded wombs and thighs.
She wouldn't leave my canvas
peering out from oceans and skies.

So I turned to poetry and feelings
only poets understand
but the dreaded verse still rhymed with eyes and thighs.

I found her face in a poem,
those eyes staring back at me
like the Lady holding the mirror to the unicorn.

For a decade the Unknown Woman danced
in my empty halls merging with light.
Her laughter echoed between the stained glass.

Her steps in circles across the floor
traced a sacred mandala refusing to hold still.

She leaves clues in the objects she holds.
Objects scatter around her feet
like Dürer's Melancholia I:
a fish, a nipple, a vacuum cleaner hose.

Every painting a new object,
a fresh set of eyes waiting.

Eyes hoping I will find her in the next
tube of paint.

A Strange Precession

A stray dog follows the other guests
around the windmill. Sleepwalkers grin
along the parade route, where
shadows stream behind comets
like the lovers of Marilyn Monroe.

My heart keeps time to a carrousel
of movie stars even though
one slips from view.

A piano player sings something Egyptian
as though she knows the words.

*I'm devoted to my art
as a spiritual channel,* she says.

Orion shows up to take our order.
We laugh knowing it will be 72 more years
until dessert arrives.

But that's the beauty of curved space,
eventually we'll invent silent-films
all over again
and go to the Texas State Fair
for another first time.

Hope Between Chaos

A white crane lifts against a grey
sky like hope
between thoughts and borrowed lines
between the crop circles appearing in my unharvested mind.

She calls consciousness and soul into one
where sea and sand disappear
between low hanging clouds.

I look away and fragments of time dip into eternity
between chaos and faith
between rocket launchers and hungry children
between what could have been and what may be.

A white crane lifts against a grey sky.

Acknowledgments

Acknowledgments are due to the editors of the following publications in which some of these poems first appeared: "Saint-Rémy de Provence" (*Pirene's Fountain* 2014), "Mirrors" (*Spirit First* 2014), "Self-Portrait" (Silver Birch Press 2014), "Painting with Turpentine and a Rag", "Slipping on Wet Paint" (*Synesthesia Literary Journal* 2014), "Participation Mystique" (*San Diego Poetry Annual* 2014-15), "Hope Between Chaos" (*The Poetry Box* 2015), "The Secret Language of Irises" (St. Julian Press), "Painting Between Shores", "Finding My Way on a Flat Canvas", "Hope Between Chaos" (*Cadence Collective*), "Both Sides of Beauty" (*Woman in Metaphor*, Natural Healing House Press 2013).

I would like to thank Russell Thorburn for his editorial and compellation assistance; Pascale Petit for her input with "Raised by a Woman in Disguise", "Crown of Honeycomb", and "Canal du Midi"; and Lois P. Jones for "Saint-Rémy de Provence". My unending appreciation goes to Maria Elena B. Mahler—the embodiment of the Feminine and the source of my inspiration.

About the Author

Stephen Linsteadt is a painter, poet, and writer. He is the author of the book, *Scalar Heart Connection*, which is concerned with humanity's connection or lack thereof with Nature, the Earth, and the global community. He has published articles about metaphysics and consciousness in *Elephant Journal, Whole Life Times, Awaken, Truth Theory*, and others. His poetry is published in *Self-Portrait Poetry Collection* (Silver Birch Press), *Synesthesia Literary Journal, Pirene's Fountain, Saint Julian Press, San Diego Poetry Annual, Moments of the Soul* (Spirit First), and others. Stephen's paintings have appeared in *Reed Magazine, Badlands Literary Journal, Birmingham Arts Journal*, and on the covers of various poetry collections.

Glass Lyre Press

exceptional works to replenish the spirit

Glass Lyre Press is an independent literary publisher interested in technically accomplished, stylistically distinct, and original work. Glass Lyre seeks diverse writers that possess a dynamic aesthetic and an ability to emotionally and intellectually engage a wide audience of readers.

Glass Lyre's vision is to connect the world through language and art. We hope to expand the scope of poetry and short fiction for the general reader through exceptionally well-written books, which evoke emotion, provide insight, and resonate with the human spirit.

Poetry Collections
Poetry Chapbooks
Select Short & Flash Fiction
Anthologies

www.GlassLyrePress.com

www.ingramcontent.com/pod-product-compliance
Lightning Source LLC
Chambersburg PA
CBHW021448080526
44588CB00009B/745